Alkaline Diet for Beginners

Alkaline diet for weight loss with food program,
to regain a healthy balance of the body with alkaline foods and lose weight quickly.

Table of Content

Introduction

Congratulations on purchasing your copy of the Alkaline Diet Book. I'm delighted that you have chosen to take a new path using the Alkaline Diet Plan to improve health, fight severe diseases like diabetes, cancer, and arthritis, weight loss and prepare healthy meals to flush away your toxins in the body.

The alkaline diet is quite healthy, encouraging a high consumption of fruits, vegetables, and healthy plant foods while restricting processed junk foods.
On the Alkaline diet, it is recommended to get 80% of Alkalizing food and the remaining 20 percent acid-forming foods. Keto diet is an excellent tool for weight loss. More importantly, it reduces risk factors for chronic diseases like hypertension, stroke, kidney stones, and more.

Meal prep is the fine way to do so — plan your food (even snacks!), so you don't find yourself achieving for too much sodium, unhealthy fats, and other additives food in a pinch. If you could commit to a couple of hours in keeping with a week on meal prep, you'll store limitless hours in the week on purchasing, cooking and selecting meals
Eating whole, unprocessed foods means eating lots of fiber-packed veggies, fruits, and beans, which boost satiety (that satisfied feeling signaling you've had enough), so you shouldn't be hungry on this diet.

In chapter 4, you will find out how a few simple food substitutions and additions can correct your acid-base woes and steer your diet in the direction of good health. Of course, to get the full benefits of the Alkaline Diet, it is also essential to include a prog of regular exercise, get a sufficient amount of quality sleep, hydrate, and include daily stress-reducing activities in your schedule.

Recipes in this book will offer you with an estimated preparation and cooking time, amount of servings, and a list of nutritional values including the net carbohydrates, protein, fats, and calories according to daily macronutrient amount. There are plenty of books on the alkaline diet and meal preparation, thanks again for choosing this book.

Chapter 1: What is the Alkaline Diet?

The human frame is supposed to maintain a carefully regulated pH stability by means of doing away with extra acid. The Typical American Regime concentrations mainly on things like white flour, sugar, animal products, and alcohol. Our bodies can hold a definite quantity of these foods, but when we overeat acidifying items and don't eat enough of the foods that support our body's ability to neutralize the acid, we become imbalanced. The body is, at times, unable to eliminate excess acid in order to maintain an optimal balance. Some professionals be certain of that it's this inequity that leads to numerous illnesses and diseases.

The Alkaline Diet stresses foods that encourage alkalinity in the blood and urine. These foods include fruits, vegetables, and certain whole grains. This regime stabilise acidifying foods and alkalizing foods, so that the body utilise more efficiently.

What is Ph?

The pH scale is used to determine whether water-based mixtures are acidic, basic, or neutral in chemistry,

A substance that is neither acidic nor primary is impartial. The pH scale, starting from 0 to 14, measures how acidic or fundamental a substance is. Greater amounts mean a material is extra alkaline (for our functions, "basic" and "alkaline" imply the same issue) or simple, and decrease numbers suggest that the substance is extra acidic.

A pH of 7 is neutral.

A pH less than 7 is acidic.

A pH greater than 7 is alkaline.

Some foods included in the Alkaline Diet may have an acidic pH (like lemons), but have an alkalizing effect on the body. So, you can't simply determine whether to eat a certain food just by looking at its pH level (more on this later). To help you sort through this, this book includes extensive food charts. By the time you've read the alkaline diet, you'll have an excellent feel of what meals to consume and which of them to keep away from.

Alkaline Water

The term alkaline water refers to the pH level of the water. Anything that is alkaline has a pH of over 7. So, if the pH of the water is 7.5, you can say its alkaline water. If it's 6, it's not alkaline water. And, like many terms that have scientific roots, alkaline water has been quickly adopted by the advertising crowd. There are many water-alkalizing contraptions available for sale, as well as bottled alkaline water. But is it necessary?

Most water is actually neutral, with a pH of 7. However, a lot depends on the water's source. Some cities have water that is slightly acidic, and others have slightly alkaline water.

There is no evidence that alkaline water affects the alkalinity of your blood or urine, which is what this diet focuses on.

Researchers Jamie A. Koufman and Nikki Johnston, in the Annals of Otology, Rhinology & Laryngology, have shown that consuming high pH water with a pH of 8.8 reduces acid reflux. If you suffer from acid reflux, this might be worth a try. The alkaline water may neutralize the acid balance in your stomach to help reduce acid reflux.

As to whether or not you need to drink water that is specifically alkalized, there's no real reason to do so. Regular filtered water is sufficient to hydrate your body and keep your organs healthy.

How Food Affects Your Body

The way most people in the Western world eat results in excess acid production after the food is broken down. The result is that the urine can become slightly too acidic, which indicates an overload of acid. Not enough to kill us, but enough to cause an imbalance that can lead to disease.

This happens as a result of foods that are too high in fat, protein, and sugars. When your body metabolizes these foods, acid by-products form. As you might remember from high school chemistry—or from popping antacids when you feel heartburn— the way to neutralize acid is to combine it with a base. So, to reduce the acid burden, your body uses alkaline minerals to link to the excess acid so the body can eliminate the acid. In a healthy person, the system works to keep the body in a slightly alkaline range (a pH of 7.30 to 7.40). If your diet is very imbalanced, with too much acid and not enough alkalizing minerals, the body can't eliminate the acid by-products. They build up in the cells of your organs and reduce the efficiency and effectiveness of your body's function.

It's not just the foods we eat. Pollution, viruses, bacteria, and health problems add extra strain on our bodies. To combat the physical stressors, the body releases stress hormones, such as cortisol, adrenaline, and insulin. Your body reacts by slowing digestion. The result is that the food you eat sits longer in your stomach and isn't digested well. So, your body doesn't obtain the optimum amount of nutrients from the food to help it rebuild and repair.

Eating too much acid-producing food wreaks real havoc on your entire body. It has to work harder to maintain a healthy pH balance. Doing so depletes the body's reserves of important minerals and causes the release of stress hormones that affect the body and the mind—not to mention the weight gain and other health problems that arise from consumption of the Ordinary American Diet.

Why Alkaline Diet Help

For the body to effectively maintain its slightly alkaline balance, it needs a rich supply of alkalizing minerals. And, we need to eat foods that don't overwhelm the body's natural ability to get rid of acid.

The Alkaline Diet works in two ways:

It eliminates foods that have an acidifying effect on your body. It adds nutrients that help repair your body. In research available in the Journal of Environmental and Public Health, researcher Gerry K. Schwal fenberg initiates that an alkaline diet leads to in a number of health benefits, some of which include:

1. The increased amounts of fruits and vegetables in an alkaline diet improve the body's potassium-sodium ratio. This may benefit bone health and muscle tone, and lessen other chronic illnesses, like hypertension and stroke.

2. An alkaline diet can help slow the natural loss of muscle mass that comes with aging.

3. Many alkaline foods are rich in magnesium, a mineral that activates vitamin D, which benefits our bones, kidneys, and hearts, among other things.

If you're recovering from an illness or chronic condition, the Alkaline Diet will infuse your body with much-needed nutrition to start the healing process, and it removes the additional stressors that a bad diet can create.

For instance, according to the National Institutes of Health, diet is one of several factors that can contribute to kidney stone formation. Kidney stones can form while substances within the urine—such as calcium and phosphorus—become enormously concentrated. Afterward, the body usages what it needs from the food we eat for rebuilding, the waste foodstuffs in the circulation are passed to the kidneys and emitted as urine.

It makes sense, then, that if our diet minimizes these harmful substances and the kidneys don't have to work as hard to balance the acid-alkaline level in your body, they'll be able to avoid kidney stones. Also, if your thyroid isn't busy handling stress hormones released because of the food you eat, it will be better able to function. Our thyroids regulate many of the hormones in the body, including those that affect our metabolism. In this way, you can achieve and sustain a healthy immune system and overall health.

The 80/20 Rule

Eighty percent of your food should come from the "Go" list of alkalizing foods.However, throughout The Essential Alkaline Diet Cookbook, you'll find information that indicates when certain foods should be "part of your 20 percent." This means it's okay to include some mildly acidic foods in your diet, but they shouldn't be more than 20 percent of your overall diet. Those recipes alert you, so it will be easy to stay on track.

How to Fallow the Alkaline Diet

By now, you may be convinced that the Alkaline Diet is the way to go. But what does it actually look like every day? What will you actually eat? Remember that the aim of the Alkaline Diet is twofold:

1. To eliminate or reduce foods that cause a buildup of acid in the body.

2. To add foods high in important minerals that help your body alkalize itself.

Following are some tips for success:

Eat at least two c of alkaline greens (kale, mustard or turnip greens, collards, or endive) daily. Lettuce is fine, but not in place of alkaline greens. Grated daikon radish is a wonderful alkalinizing condiment.

Add miso and seaweed to soups and other dishes as both a digestive aid and an alkalizer. You can also find seaweed snacks in most grocery stores and markets these days. These crunchy treats are delicious, and they add beneficial alkalizing minerals to your diet.
Eat more alkalizing grains like oats, quinoa, and wild rice. Enjoy liberal amounts of fresh fruits, especially watermelon.

Chapter 2: Advantages of Alkaline Food

Health Conditions Improved By Eating More Alkaline Diet:

A study in the Journal of Nutrition in UK concludes that "the to be had studies makes a
The compelling case that weight-reduction plan-precipitated acidosis is an actual phenomenon has full-size scientific relevance can also in large part be avoided through dietary adjustments and must be diagnosed and treated." Here are a few conditions the Alkaline Diet can assist save you.

Hypertension, stroke, and heart disorder According to the Centers for Disease Control and Prevention, over 33 percent of adults have excessive blood stress, a circumstance that will increase the risk of heart disease and stroke. While there are some of the threat factors for high blood pressure and heart disease, inclusive of inaction and being overweight, there's a clear and awesome link between what you eat and your chance. According to research published in Clinical Nutrition, the Standard American Diet, deficient in fruits and veggies and containing excessive animal merchandise, induces metabolic acidosis, and low urine ph. This high dietary acid load is more likely to result in hypertension and may also increase the hazard for hypertension and heart disease.

Bottom Line: The Alkaline Diet is excessive in the minerals potassium and magnesium, which promote healthy blood stress. Eating greater alkalizing ingredients can definitely shift your mineral ratio and may lower your chance for coronary heart sickness.

As reported by the National Kidney Foundation kidney stones, 1 in 10 humans will increase kidney Stones over the direction of a lifetime. While there are some of the threat factors, a weight loss prog high in animal protein, sodium, and sugar may also drastically increase your hazard by means of including greater "stone selling "nutrients than your kidneys can filter. This is especially true with a high-sodium eating regimen, which increases the amount of calcium your kidneys should filter.

Stone promoters, such as calcium, oxalate (positive nuts, chocolate), sodium, phosphorus, and uric acid (animal proteins), contribute to low-grade metabolic acidosis in the body. And while a young, healthful person can commonly clear out these stone promoters, as we age, we revel in a regular decline in kidney function. Passing a kidney stone is no picnic, and now the latest studies published inside the magazine Urological Research has shown that dietary acid load is the satisfactory predictor of stone formation. Bottom Line: Adding extra alkalizing, nutrient-wealthy foods for your eating regimen can lessen the accumulation of stone promoters.

Muscle mass as we age, we evidently lose muscle tissues, and extra, so if we lead an inactive lifestyle. Fewer muscle groups way we burn fewer calories in the course of the day, contributing to the "weight creep "that the majority revel in as they age. More importantly, dropping muscular tissues makes us greater liable to falls and fractures and a lack of independence. Have a study published within the American Journal of Clinical Nutrition observed that an alkaline-rich weight loss prog excessive in the end result and veggies reduced internet Acid load in elderly adults, resulting in the protection of muscles. Bottom Line: We all need to maintain our independence as we age, and adding a serving of fruits and greens to every one of your meals can assist.

Type 2 diabetes The Centers for Disease Control and Prevention estimates that about 10 percentage of the person US population has type 2 diabetes, a metabolic disorder that reasons your blood sugar to rise higher than ordinary and in which your cells grow to be proof against the movement of the hormone insulin to bring it to lower back into balance. Type 2 diabetes is basically preventable, and the latest studies have discovered that nutritional the acid load is related to the extended threat. In a study published in Diabetologia in 2013, researchers conducted a 14-12 month's cohort look at analyzing dietary facts accrued from a questionnaire from almost 70,000 French ladies.

From the responses, the researchers calculated the potential renal acid load (PRAL) and discovered a fashion correlating an excessive nutritional acid load to an accelerated risk for kind 2 diabetes. Bottom Line: In conjunction with maintaining a healthy weight, scientific proof shows that a nutritional pattern that emphasizes alkaline ingredients may additionally reduce the danger of kind 2 diabetes.

Cancer and chemotherapy, although weight loss prog-prompted acidosis may additionally certainly growth most cancers danger, at this time, there are many clinical studies that an alkaline diet can prevent most cancers. However, consistent with the journal Cancer, preliminary studies have proven that by ingesting more alkaline-selling ingredients, urine pH can be manipulated to optimize the effectiveness of chemotherapy capsules. If you have cancer or are present process chemotherapy, communicate in your physician and dietitian before making changes on your eating regimen. Bottom Line: The American Cancer Society recommends consuming a healthful diet with an emphasis
On plant ingredients, five to nine servings of fruits and veggies each day, and a cap on the intake of sodium, alcohol, processed meat, and beef, which is much like the Alkaline Diet.

Cancer cells tend to flourish much more quickly in acidic environments. As there is very often causes of cancer being found in late stages, everyone should offer much attention to pushing away any risk factor possible. Genetics is not something we can change, but our life choices are in our hands to decide. The first step we can take is what we put into our bodies.

This is where all components of the diet come into play. The pH of your body is altered by all that is consumed. As discussed partially earlier, it has to do with leftover ash product after food is used for energy. Your diet, having been changed, is now resulting in your body pH being more alkaline. It is healthier to be this way. Foods regularly consumed are energy inducing and body positive. Should the ash still be considered more acidic in nature, cancer cells are more likely to develop.

The alkaline diet severely cuts back on eating any kind of processed meats. This turns out to be amazingly beneficial to any alkaline dieter. Why? There is a known link connecting these foods to developing cancer. When cooking meat at high temperatures, it becomes very carcinogenic. This means the body is at an increased risk for cancer by consuming these because of what it produces under these conditions. The heat that is producing harmful byproducts is what makes this so.

Chronic low returned pain while research continues to be in its infancy, there's some evidence indicating that continual low backache improves with supplementation of alkaline minerals. A examine published in the Journal of Trace Elements in Medicine and Biology confirmed that increasing magnesium through supplementation allowed for the proper feature of enzyme systems and activation of diet D, which in turn improved lower backache. Bottom Line: If you suffer from lower back ache, following the Alkaline Diet will improve your degrees of magnesium and may ease your signs.

The Standard American Diet leaves tons to be desired, leaving the frame shortchanged on many Essential nutrients and minerals. Left unchecked, in the quick time period, those shortages could make you experience worn-out, disrupt your sleep, wreak havoc to your temper and concentration, and cause weight benefit. In a long time, food plan imbalances can lead to persistent sicknesses like high blood strain, type 2 diabetes, coronary heart disease, and kidney stones. Feeding your body with a mix of nutrient-dense meals on a daily

Chapter 3: Guideline to Develop Alkaline Diet

What's in your fridge? You must assess your starting point. Unhealthy habits should be easy to spot. Often times, they are the things we tend to avoid or compensate later for. You know these things are bad for you, but even so you continue to consume them. They're just that good, but for this diet to work you must let them go. Some items on this diet most aren't aware are very acidic.

Our first step is to acquaint yourself with foods that are alkaline. Then, see how many of these foods are safe for you to regularly eat. Gathering these foods and exchanging them for acidic ones is a part of this process. Most vegetables are very high in alkalinity making them a perfect choice. Don't be afraid to include them as much as possible! A variety of seeds are open to consumption as well to add to your prepared meals.

Simple alkaline meals towards the end of this book can be a wonderful guide as to what alkaline cooking is like. This diet can be started at any time with a simple trip to the store which is a great convenience.

This diet holds one of many great conveniences. It's a great first step for any beginner and is a simple purchase to make. Alkaline water has many beneficial properties and is a great replacement for soft drinks, which are high in acidity. The caloric value for a single soda bottle can range from eighty-nine calories to as high as two hundred and sixty-four. However, alkaline water has natural content in every bottle. What makes alkaline water different than regular water? Alkaline has a higher pH than your average water. This alkaline water benefits those who suffer with high blood pressure, high cholesterol, and diabetes. In addition, it also betters the efficiency in which blood flows through the veins. Its natural content contains many minerals, and it remains quite accessible to most with a nearby grocery store.

Gradual commitment is encouraged to beginners. Acquainting yourself with the new, recommended foods may be harder for those accustomed to acidic foods. Change occurs with time and your respective pace is equally important. However, this diet is full of easy to make, delicious meals. You'll have made the switch by no time! A mixture of shakes, salads, and other wonderful items will cover your days. Mealtime will soon become the next best thing. Simple things are needed to complete the items listed previously. A blender, mixing bowls, and a stove, which is almost always present in any home, is mostly all that is needed to prepare the food required of this diet. There are simple, affordable options out there for those who worry about how this will affect their budget. Adding lemon juice to water and drinking it is alkalizing enough for the body. In seconds, you are accomplishing the goal to this diet. How easy is that?

Foods to Eat

The alkaline diet will allow you to lose weight, improve your gut health, reduce your risk of diabetes and even allow you to reduce the risk for things like osteoporosis and fragile bones. It will allow you the chance to be able to reduce health risks and can help you to live a healthier and happier life. It will also allow you the chance to reset your body's abilities and give you the chance to be able to have a healthier outlook on life. Because of the way that the alkaline diet works, it is intended for your body and for making you feel better.

Some of the best foods that you can eat that are alkaline are:

- Raw food
  - Seafood
  - Meat that is up to safety standards
  - Uncooked protein sources
- Plant proteins
  - Beans
  - Legumes
  - Peanuts

- o   Quinoa
- o   Whole grains
- o   Couscous
- Fresh fruits and vegetables
  - o   Leafy greens
  - o   Peppers
  - o   Tomatoes
  - o   Eggplant
  - o   Watermelon
  - o   Berries
  - o   Carrots
  - o   Apples
- Alkaline water
- Green drinks
  - o   Greens
  - o   Fresh leafy vegetables
  - o   Water

By eating all of these foods, you will be able to get the nutrition that you need to be able to survive. You will not lack in anything – you will get protein, healthy fat and natural carbs. It will give you the chance to reset your body, and you will not have to worry about missing out on any nutrition like some of the other diets that are available, and that can help you to lose the same amount of weight. There are many different varieties of things that you can eat with the alkaline diet, and you will not feel deprived.

This is an especially good diet for people who have not been successful at diets in the past. Because you do not need to worry about cutting out any of the food groups that are in the normal eating patterns, you can have a better chance at being able to succeed with the diet. There are so many different foods that you can eat while you are on the alkaline diet that there is no chance that you will be able to be deprived of any type of food. By doing this, you will be successful on the alkaline diet and with the different options that are included with it.

There are many different options for people who want to do the alkaline diet. You can try different foods, add different things to your diet and replace some of the things with your diet. This will give you a chance to be able to increase the way that you eat and will allow you to live a healthy lifestyle.

One of the best parts of the alkaline diet is that you do not have to diet for just a short period of time. You can use the alkaline diet for the rest of your life and be able to stay as healthy as possible.

Foods to Avoid

While the alkaline foods are ones that will be able to make your health better and your weight melt away, you will be able to enjoy your life. If you start to eat acidic foods again, you will automatically notice the effects that come from them. They can make you feel sluggish, tired and you will gain the weight that you lost back. For this reason, it is a good idea to not introduce these things back into your diet until you are sure that you can eat them within reason and that you can only eat very small portions of them.

It is a good idea to avoid these foods at all costs when you are first doing the diet. Avoid them until you are satisfied with your weight loss, your gut health and your ability to live a happier lifestyle. It is a good idea to stay away from these foods and to make sure that you are getting the most out of your alkaline diet and that you are going to be as healthy as possible. These foods are all things that are sometimes considered "healthy" on other diets, but they are not good for your body if you are trying to avoid the acidity in other foods.

There are many different options that you can choose from in the foods that you can eat. You should not feel deprived just from cutting these foods out of your diet but, doing it slowly will allow you to have the best transition possible. You may not want to cut each of these foods out at once so that you can have a better chance at transitioning and not feel like you are missing out on anything.

Foods that are acidic:

- Foods high in sodium
- Eggs

- Lentils
- Dairy products
- Milk
- Yogurt
- Cheese
- Milk products
- Conventional meats that have been processed
- Lunch meat
- Turkey
- Ham
- Bologna – stay far away from this "meat."
- Hot dogs
- Premade hamburgers
- Peanuts
- Oats
- White bread
- Processed bread
- Most whole wheat save for a select few
- Gluten
- Pasta
- Rice
- Packaged grains
- Caffeine
- Alcohol

The foods that are on this list are sometimes regarded as healthy foods, and that is where most of the other diets fail at. They have people eating these foods when, in reality, they are the foods that are causing problems for the person who is doing the diet. Not only are they causing the person to not be able to lose weight, but they may also actually be causing people who are doing the diets to gain weight instead of losing it. This is something that is different depending on the type of diet that they are doing.

When it comes to the alkaline diet, the chances are that neutral foods will not hurt you too much even in the beginning. The problem comes, though, when you are eating acidic foods. They can make the body have a bad reaction and can make things harder for you when you are trying to lose weight. Each of the foods on this list can cause you to gain weight, have an unhealthy gut and not be able to get the full effects of a healthy diet.

How to Get Started Right Now

There are a lot of things that you will need to do before you jump into a diet doing all of the different things that you can do to make changes. This is something that you must take into consideration, and you must think about before you start a diet. Figure out what you want to do, the types of foods that you are going to eat and the way that you want to do the diet. Having a game plan for your alkaline diet will allow you the chance to make sure that you are able to be as successful as possible and that you will be able to eat foods that are all alkaline bases. Doing this will also prepare you for a healthier lifestyle and will give you the best opportunity possible at getting what you need.

There are a few small changes that you can make that will make it easier for you to do the diet for a long period of time:

- Add more fruits and vegetables to each of your meals
- Swap some of your carbohydrates that are processed for ones that are unprocessed – like sweet potatoes in place of French fries
- Eliminate milk from your diet

- Increase the number of raw meals that you eat each day – consider trying different things that will allow you the chance to get a better grip on what raw eating means...it's not all about sushi!
- Try something new! Consider food that is a fruit, vegetable or bean that you may not have tried in the past. This will allow you to see that there is other food out there. The more exciting things you add to your diet, the lower the chance of becoming bored with your eating choices and what is available to you
- Drink more water – aim for drinking one extra glass of water per day. Once you smash that goal, consider adding another glass of water. It would be very hard for you to drink too much water. You can also swap a different drink such as one that is caffeinated, each day for water
- Find recipes for green drinks. You can make these on your own, find mixes or even use a smoothie maker to be able to make them. Consider adding fruit for a splash of flavor in the drink

No matter what you are doing, however small it is, you are making progress toward being able to complete the alkaline diet successfully. You should make sure that you are trying your best to get the most out of the diet and that you are making the changes you need to get to a more successful point with the alkaline diet. It is all about the choices that you make and how many bases you have in your food selection.

Chapter 4: Breakfast

Good Morning Popeye

This dish is easy to prepare the night earlier than (up until the cooking step) so that you can reduce down on prep time within the morning. Since it handiest takes approximately 10 mins of actual cooking time, you may have a home-cooked breakfast any day of the week! For even quicker instruction, you may pop the candy potatoes inside the microwave for 2 to a few mins to par-cook dinner. Or, in case you opt for, integrate the components in a baking dish and bake at 350°F for 30 minutes while getting dressed and equipped to go away the residence.

- Recipe Tip Keep a bag of chopped onions for your freezer so that you can get just degree out what you want. You don't even want to defrost them; only upload the
- 1 tsp. garlic powder

Method:

1. ½ tsp. Bouquet Garni herb mixture, or different dried herbs along with rosemary or sage ½ tsp. sea salt
2. 2In a medium bowl, combine the oil, candy potatoes, onion, purple bell pepper, mushrooms, garlic, spinach, onion powder, garlic powder, Bouquet Garni, and salt. Toss till the oil and seasonings are disbursed frivolously at the greens.
3. 3Heat a non-stick frying pan over medium warmness and add the contents of the bowl. Cook the veggies, stirring, for 10 minutes, or till soft.

4. 4Three.   Divide into two portions and serve.

Serves 2. Time required for total preparation: 5 minutes. Time required for thorough cooking:: 10 minutes
m to the pan frozen.

Ingredients:
- One T coconut oil
- Two medium candy potatoes, peeled and cubed
- One medium candy onion, chopped
- One pink bell pepper, cored, seeded, and chopped
- ¼   c sliced mushrooms, any type
- Two garlic cloves, chopped
- 4 c spinach
- 1 tsp. onion powder

Each serving has an estimated (½ finished recipe): calories: 181 / total fat: 1.5g / carbohydrates: 37.8g / fiber: 8.1g / protein: five.6g

Garden pancakes

Feel free to replacement any vegetables you like on this recipe. Just make certain to pick ones that aren't too high in water content (like tomatoes), or the pancakes will crumble. Since these aren't certain with egg, be very careful whilst you turn them over. Serve these savory pancakes with salsa as opposed to syrup.

Recipe Tip You could make your own almond flour via grinding raw almonds in a meals processor.

Ingredients:

- 1 medium zucchini, kind of chopped
- 1 carrot, peeled and more or less chopped
- 1 yellow squash, more or less chopped
- ½ small onion, grated
- 4 scallions
- ¼ c almond flour 1 tsp. sea salt
- ½ tsp. garlic powder
- ¼ c filtered water, as wished Cooking spray for greasing the pan

Method:

1. Place the zucchini, carrot, yellow squash, onion, scallions, almond flour, salt, and garlic powder in a meals processor. Pulse till mixed.
2. Add the most effective sufficient water to make the aggregate wet, now not runny. The batter might be fairly thick.

3. Spray a big non-stick skillet or griddle with cooking spray. Set the skillet over medium-excessive heat.
4. 4When the oil is hot, use an ice cream scoop or ¼-c measure to drop the batter into the skillet. With a fork, spread the batter frivolously, urgent down on the pancakes. Cook, turning once, till properly browned on each facet, approximately five mins general.
5. 5Serve hot or at room temperature.

Serves 2. Time required for total preparation: 5 minutes. Time required for thorough cooking:: five mins

Each serving has an estimated (three pancakes): calories: 254 / total fat: 12.1g / carbohydrates: 33.4g / fiber: 7.2g / protein: 6.3g

Tropical granola

There isn't any want for sugary, processed industrial granola when you may make it healthful at domestic in few time than it takes to go to the marketplace. This version does now not have the conventional oats or sugar, however, it is full of evidently sweet and crunchy objects. Be positive to avoid the use of a normal shredded coconut because it has a number of sugar. You can find flaked unsweetened coconut in many everyday markets and maximum fitness food shops.

Recipe Tip This granola will preserve in a hermetic box for per week or so. Or make a further batch, and freeze it to have reachable for months!

Ingredients:

- 1 c flaked unsweetened coconut
- 1 c slivered almonds
- ½ c flaxseed
- ½ c raisins
- ½ tsp. cinnamon ¼ tsp. ginger ¼ tsp. nutmeg ¼ tsp. sea salt
- 1 vanilla bean, break up lengthwise and seeds scraped out ¼ c coconut oil
- ½ c unsweetened dried pineapple tidbits

Method:

1. Preheat the oven to 350°F.
2. In a medium bowl, integrate the coconut, almonds, flaxseed, raisins, cinnamon, ginger, nutmeg, salt, vanilla bean seeds, and coconut oil. Toss till properly mixed.

3. Spread the aggregate frivolously on a baking sheet and place it into the preheated oven. Bake for 15 mins, stirring every so often, till golden brown.
4. Remove from the oven and funky, without stirring.
5. Once cooled, stir in the pineapple tidbits.
6. Store in a hermetic box.

Serves 4. Time required for total preparation: 2 mins. Time required for thorough cooking:: 15 minutes

Each serving has an estimated (scant 1 c): calories: 182 / total fat: 0.3g / carbohydrates: 44g / fiber: 3.8g /protein: 2.3g

Summer fruit salad with lime and mint

There are few matters better than sitting outdoors on a stunning morning playing a cool fruit salad. Make this the night time earlier than so the mint has time to mingle with the culmination. And, as usually, sense loose to substitute any fruits you opt for. Just avoid blueberries, as they're on the "No Go" listing.

Recipe Tip If you don't have time to make this the night time before, you could make it and serve it proper away. It's scrumptious either manner.

Ingredients:

- ¼ c grapes
- ¼ c peeled and diced apple
- ¼ c chunk-size watermelon pieces
- ¼ c chew-length honeydew melon pieces
- ¼ c chunk-size cantaloupe pieces
- ¼ c tangerine slices
- ¼ c peeled and diced peaches
- ¼ c strawberries
- 2 T chopped fresh mint
- 2 T freshly squeezed lemon juice

Method:

1. In a medium bowl, combine the grapes, apple, watermelon, honeydew, cantaloupe, tangerine, peaches, and strawberries.
2. Add the mint and lemon juice. Mix properly to combine. Cover and refrigerate in a single day.
3. Spoon into four bowls, and serve chilled.

Serves 4. Time required for total preparation: 10 minutes

Each serving has an estimated (½ c): calories: 32 / total fat: 0.02g / carbohydrates: 7.8g / fiber: zero.09g /protein: zero.6g

Winter fruit compote with figs and ginger

This recipe is the wintry weather equal to a summertime fruit salad. It's basically a heat fruit stew that is comforting and healthful on a cold wintry weather morning. Feel free to add unique culmination you opt for. This is also amazing for dessert.

Recipe tip this is also scrumptious served cold. Top it with Coconut Whipped Cream for a delicious and healthy dessert.

Ingredients:

- 2 small tangerines, peeled and sectioned
- 1 apple, peeled, cored, and diced
- ½ c figs stemmed and quartered
- ½ c dried plums (prunes), halved ¼ c dark cherries
- 1 c of filtered water
- 1 vanilla bean, cut up lengthwise and seeds scraped out
- 1 tsp. grated clean ginger
- ½ tsp. cinnamon
- ½ tsp. cloves
- 1 packet stevia (non-compulsory)

Method:

1. In a medium saucepan, combine the tangerines, apple, figs, dried plums, cherries, water, vanilla bean seeds, ginger, cinnamon, cloves, and stevia (if the use of).
2. Bring to a simmer over medium warmness and prepare dinner, occasionally stirring, for 10 mins, or until the fruit is soft but not too smooth. Remove from the heat.

3. Let stand for 30 minutes to meld the flavors.
4. Reheat if important, spoon into 4 bowls and serve heat.

Serves four. Time required for total preparation: 10 minutes. Time required for thorough cooking:: 10 mins

Each serving has an estimated (1 c): calories: 102 / total fat: 0.4g / carbohydrates: 26g / fiber: four.2g /
Protein: 1g

All-American apple pie

Imagine the looks on your youngsters' faces while you tell them they are able to have apple pie for breakfast. Of direction, this apple pie is healthful! Since that is a breakfast recipe, this version is crust less. But in case you need to make it for dessert, use the recipe for All-Purpose Pie Crust (right here) and pinnacle with some Coconut Ice Cream (right here).

Recipe Tip You can use any form of apples for this pie. Generally speaking, inexperienced apples hold their shape higher than other kinds while cooked. But use your favored here and enjoy.

Ingredients:

- 4 Golden Delicious apples, peeled, cored, and sliced
- ½ c freshly squeezed orange juice
- 1 vanilla bean, split lengthwise and seeds scraped out
- ¼ tsp. cinnamon
- Unsweetened coconut milk, as wanted (optional)

Method:

1. In a massive bowl, toss the apples with the orange juice, vanilla bean seeds, and cinnamon.
2. In a medium skillet set over medium warmness, upload the fruit mixture. Cook for 10 minutes, or until the apples are smooth and caramelized.
3. Divide the combination amongst 4 serving dishes, and serve warm.
4. Top with coconut milk (if the use of).

Serves 4. Time required for total preparation: 10 mins. Time required for thorough cooking:: 10 mins

Each serving has an estimated (1 c): calories: 109 / total fat: 0.1g / carbohydrates: 28.5g / fiber: four.5g /Protein: 0.2g

Baby potato home fries

Who wishes the high-fats, high-sodium restaurant model of domestic fries? Instead, this healthy model uses infant white potatoes and a non-stick pan to offer you all of the flavors without the acid-producing facet results. If you have got leftovers, you could relax them and make a potato salad. Its breakfast or lunch!

Recipe Tip You also can use small pink potatoes for this recipe. It's great to avoid the brown russet potatoes commonly used for baking as they include a number of starch.

Ingredients:

- 4 medium infant white potatoes
- 2 oz. vegetable broth
- ½ sweet white onion, chopped
- 1 red bell pepper, seeded and diced
- ½ c sliced mushrooms
- 1 tsp. of sea salt
- 1 tsp. garlic powder

Method:

1. In a medium microwave-secure bowl, microwave the potatoes for 4 mins, or till gentle. Let cool.
2. In a big non-stick skillet set over medium warmness, upload the broth, onion, and purple bell pepper. Sauté the vegetables for approximately 5 mins, or till gentle.
3. While the onion and peppers cook dinner, reduce the potatoes into quarters.
4. Add the potatoes, mushrooms, salt, and garlic powder to the skillet. Stir to combine. Cook until the potatoes are crisp.

5.   Serve heat.

Serves 2. Time required for total preparation: five minutes. Time required for thorough cooking:: 20 minutes

Each serving has an estimated (1 c): calories: 337 / total fat: zero.8g / carbohydrates: 74.8g / fiber: 12.4g /protein: 9.3g

Breakfast fajitas

This eating place staple can effortlessly be tailored as a brilliant breakfast meal. It's a superb manner to load up on healthful greens and fill your stomach to start your day. Wrap these fajitas in lettuce leaves, if you desire. However, they may be extraordinary just eaten hot from the skillet with a fork.

Recipe Tip There is a source hyperlink in the Resources phase for coconut-flour tortillas.

Wrap one of these round those fajitas for a filling breakfast.

Ingredients:

- Cooking spray
- 1 bell pepper, any colour, cored, seeded, and sliced
- 1 candy onion, including Vidalia, chopped
- 1 c cooked broccoli florets
- ½ c sliced mushrooms
- 1 c cherry tomatoes, halved if huge
- ½ c sliced zucchini, or other squash
- 2 garlic cloves, peeled and chopped
- 1 jalapeño, chopped (non-obligatory)
- 1 tsp. of sea salt
- ½ tsp. cumin
- 2 T fresh cilantro
- Juice of ½ lime
- Salsa Fresca (right here), for serving

Method:

1. Spray a massive non-stick skillet with cooking spray and place it over medium warmth.
2. Add the bell pepper, onion, broccoli, mushrooms, tomatoes, zucchini, garlic, and jalapeño (if the use of). Cook, stirring, for about 7 minutes, or till the favored degree of tenderness.
3. Three.   Stir in the salt, cumin, and cilantro. Cook, stirring, for 3 mins greater.
4. Remove from warmth and upload the lime juice.
5. Divide among two plates and serve with Salsa Fresca.
6. Serves 2. Time required for total preparation: five mins. Time required for thorough cooking:: 10 minutes

Each serving has an estimated (½ finished recipe): calories: 86 / total fat: 0.07g / carbohydrates: 17.4g /
Fiber: five.1g / protein: four.1g

Grandma's baked grapefruit

Grapefruit is notable at any temperature, but it's miles specifically precise baked. This diet C-wealthy fruit is filled with fiber and nutrition. When baked, it's typically topped with brown sugar or maple syrup, but this model uses grated coconut instead. Make this warming breakfast on a cold day.

Recipe Tip Ruby Red is a diffusion of grapefruit that has a tendency to be sweeter than other sorts. If you're not a big grapefruit fan, attempt Ruby Red first.

Ingredients:

- 1 grapefruit, halved
- 2 T grated unsweetened coconut

Method:

1. Preheat the oven to 350°F.

2. Place the grapefruit halves on a foil-lined baking pan. Top every half with 1 T of coconut.

3. Place the pan within the preheated oven and bake for 15 mins, or till the coconut is browned.

4. Serve the grapefruit halves on a plate and devour with a spoon.

Serves 1. Time required for total preparation: 15 mins. Time required for thorough cooking:: 15 minutes

Each serving has an estimated: calories: 86 / total fat: 0.07g / carbohydrates: 11.9g / fiber: 2.3g / protein: 1.2g

Breakfast parfait

Breakfast parfait

This version of a fruit parfait is so clean to make you're going to surprise why you never made it before. Instead of yogurt or whipped cream, this recipe requires Coconut Whipped Cream

Recipe Tip Feel loose to switch in any fruits you like. Get bold and layer in such things as pumpkin or sweet potato!

Ingredients:

- ¼ c sliced strawberries
- ¼ c blackberries
- ¼ c sliced raspberries
- ¼ c sliced peaches
- 1 c Coconut Whipped Cream

Method:

1. In a large clean glass, region 2 T strawberries and pinnacle with 2 T whipped cream. Add 2 T blackberries and any other 2 T whipped cream. Continue with 2 T raspberries and a pair of T whipped cream. Finish with 2 T peaches and 2 T whipped cream.
2. Repeat with the remaining ingredients in a 2nd glass.
3. Serve without delay.

Serves 2. Time required for total preparation: 10 minutes

Each serving has an estimated (½ c fruit with ½ c coconut whipped cream): calories: a hundred and twenty / total fat: 10g/ carbohydrates: 4g / fiber: 6.3g / protein: 1.7g

---

Hearty breakfast sausage

While traditional sausage consists of loads of bad ingredients, this model is made with beans. Beans are one of those ingredients that need to be to your 20 percent list—meaning you have to eat them sparingly. Even so, that is a protein-rich complement to other recipes in this chapter. And, in the shape of a sausage, it's delicious, too!

Recipe Tip You can dry fry those sausage patties through cooking them in a non-stick pan sprayed with cooking spray — Fry for about five minutes in keeping with aspect
.

Ingredients:

- 2 garlic cloves
- 1 small onion, quartered
- 1 carrot, peeled and reduce into massive chunks
- ½ tsp. fennel seeds Water, as needed
- 1 (15-oz.) can pinto beans, drained
- 1 T almond flour or almond meal
- 1 T dietary yeast
- 1 tsp. smoked paprika
- ½ tsp. dried oregano (1 tsp. clean)
- ½ tsp. dried sage (1 tsp. fresh)
- ½ tsp. dried basil (1 tsp. sparkling)
- ½ tsp. dried thyme (1 tsp. fresh)
- ½ tsp. of sea salt
-

Method:

1. Preheat the oven to four 100°F.
2. Place a baking paper with a silicone mat.

3. In a meals processor, add the garlic, onion, and carrot. Chop till exceptional, or chop by means of hand.

4. Place a medium skillet over medium warmth. Add the onion-carrot combination and the fennel seeds. Cook for about four minutes or till the greens are smooth, including water if wished. Remove from the warmth and funky.

5. In the meals processor, add the pinto beans and pulse till more or less chopped, however no longer to a paste. Add the onion-carrot aggregate to the processor, and technique till combined.

6. Transfer the contents to a medium bowl. Add the almond flour, yeast, paprika, oregano, sage, basil, thyme, and salt. Mix till the components are combined.

7. Measure a ¼ c of sausage and form into a patty by using a hand. Carefully area every patty

8. Onto the organized pan. Continue with the remaining sausage.

9. Eight.   Bake for 25 to half-hour, till crispy at the outside, however nevertheless moist on the internal.

10. Take away from the stove and leave for a few minutes before serving.

Serves nine. Time required for total preparation: 20 minutes. Time required for thorough cooking:: 35 minutes

Each serving has an estimated (1 patty): calories: sixty nine / total fat: 1.7g / carbohydrates: 10.7g / fiber: 3g /protein: three.5g

Sweet potato waffles with applesauce

This recipe would possibly simply come to be your new Sunday morning lifestyle. These waffles (or pancakes, in case you don't have a waffle iron) are so healthy and delicious you received even omit the acid-producing buttermilk ones you're used to consuming. Be careful while removing them from the waffle iron, as they're extraordinarily wet and fragile. If one does disintegrate, consume it and phone it your "chef's bonus."

Recipe Tip If you don't have applesauce, serve those with Apple Butter

Ingredients:

- 1¼ c almond flour
- 2 tsp. baking powder
- ½   tsp. sea salt Dash nutmeg Dash cinnamon ⅓ c coconut oil
- 1½ c unsweetened coconut milk 1 c mashed candy potato Cooking spray
- 1 c unsweetened applesauce

Method:

1. Preheat the waffle iron.
2. In a massive bowl, integrate the almond flour, baking powder, salt, nutmeg, and cinnamon.
3. 3 In a medium bowl, whisk together the coconut oil and coconut milk until combined.
4. Transfer the liquid substances to the bowl with the dry elements. Whisk until combined.
5. Gently fold the candy potatoes into the batter, being cautious no longer to over mix.

6. Spray the waffle iron with cooking spray earlier than making every waffle.
7. Make the waffles in line with the instructions indicated on the waffle iron.
8. Serve every waffle with a ¼ c of applesauce.

Serves four. Time required for total preparation: 15 mins. Time required for thorough cooking:: five to 7 minutes

Each serving has an estimated (1 waffle with ¼ c applesauce): calories: 547 / total fat: 25g /
Carbohydrates: 38g / fiber: 16.9g / protein: 14.6g

Spaghetti squash hash browns

Who desires the high-fats, acid-generating restaurant hash browns whilst you could make those delicious and nutritious ones at home? This recipe requires cooked spaghetti squash, so the day earlier than you are making those, just pop a spaghetti squash in the oven, and roast it (be aware underneath). This way, the recipe takes only some mins to put together. Serve with Hearty Breakfast Sausage (right here) and Homemade Ketchup (here). Just bear in mind to pass the ketchup in case you're following the Thyroid-Support Plan.

Recipe Tip Make positive you squeeze as tons moisture as you may from the spaghetti squash so it will crisp.

Ingredients:

- 2 c cooked spaghetti squash
- ½ c finely chopped onion
- 1 tsp. garlic powder
- ½ tsp. of sea salt Cooking spray

Method:

1. Using a paper towel, squeeze any excess moisture from the spaghetti squash. Place the squash in a medium bowl. Add the onion, garlic powder, and salt. Mix to combine.
2. Drizzle a moderate non-stick pan with culinary spray and location it over medium heat.
3. Add the squash aggregate to the pan. Cook, untouched, for 5 mins. With a spatula, turn the hash browns. It's ok if the mixture falls apart. Cook for approximately five mins more, or until the favored level of crispness.

---

4. To roast spaghetti squash, cut the squash in 1/2 lengthwise and scrape out the seeds. Brush every half off with 2 T of coconut oil and season with 1 tsp. of sea salt. Place the squash halves cut-aspect up on a baking sheet and roast at 350°F for about 50 minutes, or till fork tender.

Serves 2. Time required for total preparation: 2 minutes. Time required for thorough cooking:: 10 mins

Each serving has an estimated (1 c): calories: 44 / total fat: zero.6g / carbohydrates: 9.7g / fiber: zero.6g /protein: zero.9g

Brown rice porridge

Brown rice and almond milk update the white rice and cow's milk historically located in this English-inspired breakfast. Feel unfastened to feature any end result you have got on hand. Bananas and a bit cinnamon will make it hearty; cherries and papaya will make it tropical. Add a hint of coconut milk or almond milk earlier than serving if the porridge is simply too thick.

Recipe Tip You can buy brown rice cereal in the market. Use it instead of ordinary brown rice on this recipe to make this alkaline-pleasant dish even faster and simpler.

Ingredients:

- Three c cooked brown rice.
- 1 c almond milk
- 1 packet stevia

Method:

1. In a medium saucepan, combine the brown rice and the almond milk. Simmer over medium warmness for 5 mins, stirring continuously, until the mixture is thick and creamy.
2. Remove from warmness. Stir within the stevia.

3. Divide amongst 6 bowls and serve.

Serves 6. Time required for total preparation: 5 mins. Time required for thorough cooking:: 5 mins

Each serving has an estimated (½ c porridge): calories: 236 / total fat: 1.8g / carbohydrates: 48.3g / fiber: 3.6g / protein: 7g

Pumpkin-spice quinoa casserole

This hearty casserole can be assembled the night earlier than baking to make morning instruction a snap. Quinoa is a protein powerhouse that adds a nutty taste. The pumpkin holds its own with tons of beta-carotene and fiber. And the use of cooked quinoa makes assembly even simpler. This breakfast is one to maintain you going all morning lengthy.

Recipe Tip You can, without a doubt, microwave this dish to make it even faster. Simply pop the combination into the microwave for 7 mins on excessive, or until the pumpkin is set.
Ingredients:

- Cooking spray
- three c cooked quinoa
- 1 (15-oz.) can pumpkin purée
- A ½ c of water
- 1 vanilla bean, break up lengthwise and seeds scraped out
- 1 tsp. cinnamon
- ½ tsp. nutmeg
- ½ tsp. floor ginger
- ¼ tsp. grated sparkling ginger
- ¼ tsp. of sea salt
- Preheat the oven to 350°F.
- Spray a 4-c casserole dish and set apart.

Method:

1. 1In a medium bowl, stir together the quinoa, pumpkin, water, vanilla bean seeds, cinnamon, nutmeg, ground ginger, fresh ginger, and salt.

66

2. 2Transfer the combination to the prepared casserole dish. Bake for 15 minutes, or till golden and bubbly.
3.

Serves 6. Time required for total preparation: 5 mins. Time required for thorough cooking:: 15 mins

Each serving has an estimated (1 c): calories: 26 / total fat: 5g / carbohydrates: 57.1g / fiber: 7.7g / protein: 12g

Chapter 5: Lunch

The Asian bowl

This first recipe in this bowl chapter is a superb example of the fundamentals of bowl assembly. The general manner to make a good bowl is to layer a grain, a bean, a vegetable, and a sauce. Of path, the recipes on this eBook simplest include substances on the authorized meals list, so grains frequently are replaced with some other vegetable. The base for this Asian Bowl is shredded cabbage. If you're in the mood for a heat bowl, sauté the cabbage and carrots first.

Recipe Tip Cashew butter is commonly placed near the peanut butter in grocery stores. If you can't find cashew butter, you could use almond butter; just make certain it doesn't have brought the sugar.

Ingredients:

- 1 c shredded inexperienced cabbage
- 1 c shredded purple cabbage
- 1 c chopped carrots
- ¼ c water chestnuts
- 3 T chopped scallions
- 1 T darkish sesame oil
- 1 T cashew butter

Method:

1. ¼ tsp. red pepper flakes, or extra as wished ½ tsp. ginger powder
2. Hot water, as wanted.
3. 2 tsp. toasted sesame seeds
4. In a medium bowl, layer the inexperienced and purple cabbage, then the carrots, water chestnuts, and scallions.
5. In a blender, upload the sesame oil, cashew butter, purple pepper flakes, and ginger powder. Blend until the substances emulsify. Add warm water, by means of the tsp., if the dressing is simply too thick.
6. Pour the dressing over the greens, add sesame seeds, and serve.

Serves 1. Time required for total preparation: 5 minutes

Each serving has an estimated: calories: 317 / total fat: 24.7g / carbohydrates: 20.8g / fiber: 6.6g / protein:7.2G

The breakup bowl

It befalls to almost everybody. You get dumped. Don't permit that derail your healthy eating plan! Instead of crying over a pint of ice cream, dump those sweet, healthful substances right into a bowl and soothe your body and your soul.

Recipe Tip You can add different end results as you like. Frozen cherries are a superb addition, as are clean strawberries.

Ingredients:

- 2 bananas, peeled, sliced, and frozen
- 2 T coconut milk
- 2 T fruit-sweetened-only strawberry jam
- 2 T grated unsweetened coconut
- 2 T chopped toasted almonds
- ¼ c Coconut Whipped Cream

Method:

1. In a food processor, vicinity the frozen bananas. Add the coconut milk and mix until they're the consistency of ice cream. Transfer to an unmarried-serving bowl.

2. Top the bananas with the jam, coconut, toasted almonds, and whipped cream.

3. Serve right away.

Serves 1. Time required for total preparation: five minutes

Each serving has an estimated: calories: 454 / total fat: 19.2g / carbohydrates: sixty-nine.4g / fiber: 9.6g / protein: 6.9g

The comfort bowl

This bowl is perfect for whilst you've had an awful day. Curl up on the couch with this heartwarming—and wholesome—dish. This is the simplest recipe inside the book that makes use of mashed potatoes. Because of this, it ought to be taken into consideration a part of your 20 percent.

Recipe Tip Depending on whether or not you want peas, you may no longer discover them comforting. If no longer, then replacement an alkaline-friendly vegetable that does comfort you, like perhaps spinach or lima beans.

Ingredients:

- 1 c cooked toddler potatoes
- 2 T almond milk
- ½ tsp. of sea salt
- ½ c inexperienced peas
- ½ c Great Gravy

Method:

1. In a medium bowl, combine the potatoes, almond milk, and salt. Mash with a fork to the preferred consistency.
2. Top the potatoes with the peas and the gravy. Warm the bowl within the microwave on excessive for 1 minute, and eat.

Serves 1. Time required for total preparation: 15 mins

Each serving has an estimated: calories: 205 / total fat: 2.4g / carbohydrates: 41.3g / fiber: 7.3g / protein: 8.1g

The fight it off bowl

This bowl is a form of dishonesty, as it's essentially a soup. But, it's a first-rate desire while you suppose you're fighting off a chilly or the flu. Make a massive bowl of this nutritious concoction, and show the one's germs that you're the boss. Your immune device will thanks.

Recipe Tip Add other greens to reinforce the healing homes if you're going to apply spinach, although, upload it no extra than 5 minutes earlier than serving.

Ingredients:

- 2 c vegetable broth
- 1 carrot, peeled and sliced
- ½ c bite-size broccoli florets
- 2 garlic cloves, finely minced

Method:

1. In a moderate pot set over moderate hotness, integrate the broth, carrot, broccoli, and garlic. Cook for 10 mins, or until veggies reach a preferred level of tenderness.
2. Pour into a bowl, and consume.

Serves 1. Time required for total preparation: 5 minutes. Time required for thorough cooking:: 10 minutes

Each serving has an estimated: calories: 126 / total fat: 2.9g / carbohydrates: 12.8g / fiber: 2.8g / protein: 11.8g

The harvest bowl

This recipe is like Thanksgiving in a bowl, however, in place of acid-producing turkey and stuffing, this bowl gives the first-rate of the autumn harvest. The combination of untamed rice, apples, sweet potatoes, and gravy is classic and delicious.

Recipe Tip Add a few inexperienced beans or mushrooms, for extra vitamins and flavor. Maybe both!

Ingredients:

- 1 c cooked brown rice
- ¼ c cooked wild rice
- 1 apple, peeled, cored, and diced
- ½   c mashed candy potato ¼ c Great Gravy

Method:

1. In a medium bowl, layer the brown rice, wild rice, apple, candy potato, and gravy.
2. Microwave on excessive for approximately 2 mins, or until warm. Serve.

Serves 1. Time required for total preparation: 10 mins

Each serving has an estimated: calories: 579 / total fat: 3.1g / carbohydrates: 45.7g / fiber: three.6g / protein: 8.9g

The Hawaiian bowl

This recipe is one of the few on this e-book that requires brown rice. Since it's at the restriction list, this bowl ought to be taken into consideration in every of your 20 percent food. The Homemade Barbecue Sauce that tops that is so delicious you may need to top the entirety with it. Feel unfastened to feature exclusive greens, as you pick out.

Recipe Tip The sauce will hold for a few days inside the fridge, or you may freeze it and it'll closing for months.

To render this recipe a preference for the Thyroid-Support Plan, replacement the Asian Citrus Dressing (right here) for the Homemade Barbecue Sauce used right here.

Ingredients:

- ½   c cooked brown rice
- 1 c steamed broccoli
- ¼ c packed-in-juice pineapple chunks, tired, liquid reserved 2 T Homemade Barbecue Sauce.

Method:

1. In a medium bowl, layer the brown rice, broccoli, and pineapple.
2. In a small saucepan set over medium warmness, whisk together the reserved pineapple juice and the Homemade Barbecue Sauce for about five mins, until thickened and bubbly.
3. Pour over the rice and broccoli and serve.

Serves 1. Time required for total preparation: 5 minutes. Time required for thorough cooking:: five minutes

Each serving has an estimated: calories: 223 / total fat: 1.6g / carbohydrates: 47.6g / fiber: 4.6g / protein: 3.6g

The Hollywood bowl

What do you suspect when you consider Hollywood? Stars! This bowl is made with famous person-fashioned food so that you'll want a star-formed cookie cutter. The recipe additionally requires a celebrity fruit that, whilst cut, is certainly within the shape of a star.

Recipe Tip Even if you don't cut the watermelon into megastar shapes, this is a delicious bowl. After all, Hollywood stars make their own guidelines!

Ingredients:

- 1 megastar fruit
- ¼ watermelon, reduce into slices
- ¼ c Coconut Whipped Cream

Method:

1. Slice the celebrity fruit into famous person-shaped pieces.
2. Press the cookie cutter into watermelon slices to create celebrity-fashioned pieces.
3. Add the megastar fruit and watermelon to a single-serving bowl. Top with the Coconut Whipped Cream.
4. Serve without delay.

Serves 1. Time required for total preparation: five mins

Each serving has an estimated: calories: a hundred twenty five / total fat: 9.6g / carbohydrates: 9.3g / fiber: 2.7g / protein: 1.8g

The Indian bowl

This scrumptious bowl begins with a layer of nutty, crunchy quinoa. It's topped with only some chickpeas, then a layer of steamed greens. Finally, a scrumptious coconut curry sauce drenches this bowl in creamy goodness.

Recipe Tip For a trade of tempo, add a few eggplants, too. Just keep in mind that doing so will make this incorrect for the ones on the Thyroid-Support Plan.

Ingredients:

- 1 c cooked quinoa, warmed
- 1 large carrot, peeled, sliced, and steamed
- ½ c cooked cauliflower florets ⅛ c chickpeas
- ¼ c sliced mushrooms
- A ½ c of coconut milk
- 1 T yellow curry powder
- ½ tsp. ground ginger
- 1 tsp. of sea salt
- 1 T tomato paste

Method:

1. In a medium bowl, layer the quinoa, carrot, cauliflower, and chickpeas.
2. In a little pot set over moderate temperature, integrate the mushrooms, coconut milk, curry powder, ginger, salt, and

tomato paste. Whisk until the aggregate simmers. Cook for five minutes after which cool barely.

3. Pour the sauce over the quinoa combination and serve immediately.

Serves 1. Time required for total preparation: 10 minutes. Time required for thorough cooking:: five mins

Each serving has an estimated: calories: 469 / total fat: 0.2g / carbohydrates: 26.1g / fiber: thirteen.5g / protein: 5.4g

The Italian bowl

This recipe has all the conventional Italian flavors without the fat-encumbered meats and sausage. Once you've made this a couple of times, experience unfastened to play around with the ingredients. Add bell peppers for sweetness, inexperienced beans or broccoli for greater vegetables, or any lawn vegetables you have on hand. Be sure to apply clean herbs, as they add the intense taste to this dish.

Recipe Tip Make a double batch and integrate the ingredients in a pot with 2 c of vegetable broth to make a hearty Italian soup. Warm over medium warmth and serve warm.

Ingredients:

- 1 (14.Five-oz.) can tomatoes, complete, diced, or crushed, undrained
- 1 medium onion, diced
- ½ c sliced zucchini
- four garlic cloves, minced ⅓ c fresh chopped basil
- ½ tsp. chopped clean oregano
- 2 T freshly squeezed lemon juice
- 1 c cooked quinoa, warmed
- ½ c eggplant, peeled, diced, cooked and rewarmed

Method:

1. Drain 2 T of liquid from the tomatoes and add it to a medium saucepan set over medium warmness. Add the onion and sauté for 5 minutes, or till translucent.

2. Add the tomatoes with their last juices, zucchini, garlic, basil, and oregano. Stir to mix. Simmer for 5 minutes. Remove from the heat and stir inside the lemon juice.
3. In a single-serving bowl, layer the quinoa and the eggplant. Top with the tomato mixture.
4. Serve warm.

Serves 1. Time required for total preparation: 5 mins. Time required for thorough cooking:: 10 mins

Each serving has an estimated: calories: 390 / total fat: 5.4g / carbohydrates: seventy one.5g / fiber: 10.8g / protein: 14.5g

The lady and the tramp bowl

This bowl is called after the classic scene in the movie Lady, and the Tramp wherein the two characters share a bowl of pasta and end up kissing. As such, this is the only bowl within the bankruptcy that serves two—kissing optional. Spaghetti squash stands in for the pasta on this dish. A layer of sparkling tomatoes and a topping of Sun-Dried Tomato Sauce (right here) make this date-worthy.

Recipe Tip Feel free to layer in any additional greens which you like. Mushrooms, spinach, or maybe broccoli could be desirable.

Ingredients:

- 2 c cooked, shredded spaghetti squash
- 1 c chopped clean tomatoes
- 1 c Sun-Dried Tomato Sauce

Method:

1. Layer the spaghetti squash and tomatoes in a bowl huge enough for 2 people. Top with the Sun-Dried Tomato Sauce.
2. In the microwave, warm the bowl for 2 mins on excessive, or till heated thru.
3. Serve with forks and plenty of napkins.

To roast spaghetti squash, cut the squash in half of lengthwise and scrape out the seeds. Brush every 1/2 with 2 T of coconut oil and season with 1 tsp. of sea salt. Place the squash halves reduce-facet up on a baking sheet and roast at 350°F for about 50 minutes, or until fork gentle.

Serves 2. Time required for total preparation: 15 mins

Each serving has an estimated (1½ c plus ½ c sauce): calories: 153 /
total fat: 4.1g / carbohydrate: 27.1g/ fiber: four.2g / protein: 3.5g

The lazy bowl

The Lazy Bowl is for those nights when you feel so lazy you don't actually have the mojo to cook dinner the best dish. This recipe relies on leftovers from other recipes. The method is straightforward: Layer 1 is a grain or root vegetable; Layer 2 is a vegetable; Layer three is a topping or sauce. The nutritional facts are calculated given the sample suggestions. Your effects will vary relying on what you include.

Recipe Tip If you realize you're going to be tremendous busy one week, make a little greater of the whole thing you cook dinner so that you have leftovers reachable to make The Lazy Bowl.

Ingredients:

- Layer One: 1 c Baby Potato Home Fries
- Layer Two: ½ c Marinated Vegetables
- Layer Three: ¼ c Healthy Hummus

Method:

1. In an unmarried-serving bowl, layer the potatoes, veggies, and hummus, and eat! Serves 1. Time required for total preparation: five minutes

Each serving has an estimated: calories: 510 / total fat: nine.9g / carbohydrates: 32.4g / fiber: 6.7g / protein: 12.8g

The Mexican bowl

Who needs to go to a Mexican speedy-food eating place to get a scrumptious and wholesome bowl? Not you! When you make this zesty bowl, you get all the taste and none of the acidifying substances that frequently include take-out fare. Add a chopped jalapeño if you like things on the highly spiced facet.

Ingredients:

- 1 c sprouted black beans
- 1 tsp. floor cumin
- 1 medium sweet potato, cooked and diced
- ½ c chopped cilantro
- ½ avocado, diced
- 3 T Salsa Fresca
- Pinch sea salt

Method:

1   In a small bowl, integrate the beans and the cumin.
2.   In a medium microwaveable bowl, layer the candy potatoes and top with the beans. Warm the veggies in the microwave on high for two minutes, or until heated through.
3.   Remove from the microwave and layer on the cilantro and avocado, and pinnacle with the Salsa Fresca.
4.   Season with the salt and serve immediately.

Serves 1. Time required for total preparation: 10 minutes

Each serving has an estimated: calories: 436 / total fat: 11.4g / carbohydrates: sixty nine.5g / fiber: 17.4g / protein: 17.8g

The rose bowl

If life is only a bowl of cherries, then this recipe is complete of lifestyles! The Rose Bowl carries all crimson ingredients in a delicious aggregate. Red meals incorporate antioxidants, which help heal the frame and prevent disease. They accomplish that with the aid of reducing the infection that may motive internal damage.

Recipe Tip if you can't discover crimson quinoa, everyday quinoa will work just as well.

Ingredients:

- 1 c cooked purple quinoa
- ½ c roasted, diced purple peppers
- ½ c darkish pink cherries pitted and sliced ¾ tsp. pink curry paste
- ½ c of coconut milk

Method:

1. In an unmarried-serving bowl, layer the quinoa, pink peppers, and cherries.
2. In a blender, mix together the curry paste and coconut milk. Pour the liquid over the layered quinoa, peppers, and cherries.
3. Microwave on high for approximately 2 mins, or till warm.

Serves 1. Time required for total preparation: five mins

Each serving has an estimated: calories: 401 / total fat: 1.8g / carbohydrates: sixty four.5g / fiber: 6.7g / protein: 16.7g

The southern bowl

Eating this bowl will make you feel like you're in the Deep South. With candy potato, southern veggies, and okra, this packs a number of vitamins into one meal. Greens normally are made with meat. However, this version tastes simply as superb with alkaline-pleasant elements. Also, in case you're now not partial to okra, deliver it a strive on this recipe besides.

Recipe Tip If you're involved that the okra will be slimy, use the frozen type.

Ingredients:

- ¼ c vegetable broth, divided
- ¼ candy onion, chopped
- 1 garlic clove, finely chopped
- ½ tsp. sea salt, divided
- 4 oz. canned diced tomatoes
- 1 c collard veggies
- 1 sliced okra, sparkling or frozen
- 1 sweet potato, peeled and cut into chunk-size pieces
- ¼ c almond milk

Method:

1. In a massive saucepan set over medium heat, warmth 2 T vegetable broth. Add the onion and sauté for five mins, or until translucent.

2. Add the garlic, ¼ tsp. salt, tomatoes, the ultimate 2 T broth, collard greens, and okra. Simmer for 30 to 35 mins, or until gentle.
3. Meanwhile, in a medium pot of boiling water, prepare dinner, the candy potato pieces for 10 mins, or until gentle. Drain and place in a medium bowl. Add the almond milk and the last ¼ tsp. salt. Using an electric powered mixer, mash the sweet potatoes.
4. Place the warm mashed sweet potato in a bowl. Top with the collard greens and okra mixture. Finish with any tomato sauce left within the pan.

Serves 1. Time required for total preparation: 10 mins. Time required for thorough cooking:: 40 minutes

Each serving has an estimated: calories: 201 / total fat: 2.7g / carbohydrates: 37.5g / fiber: 7.3g / protein: 9g

The super bowl

Although this recipe shares a name with a well-known soccer sport, it has a slightly distinctive which means. This bowl contains the handiest ingredients taken into consideration to be superfoods. These dietary powerhouse meals integrate to make this recipe high in protein, vitamins, minerals, and fiber. Choose this bowl if you're combating off a cold.

Recipe Tip Remember that the stems are a part of the kale this is bitter. If you absolutely hate kale, you may need replacement spinach.

Ingredients:

- 1 c cooked quinoa
- 1 c kale, uncooked, steamed, or sautéed
- ¼ c açaí berries
- 1 T apple cider vinegar
- 1 T coconut oil
- ¼ tsp. mustard powder
- ¼ tsp. of sea salt
- Dash garlic powder
- Dash onion powder

Method:

1. In a single-serving bowl, layer the quinoa and kale.

2. In a blender, combination the açaí berries, cider vinegar, coconut oil, mustard powder, salt, garlic powder, and onion powder till the elements emulsify.
3. Pour the dressing over the quinoa-kale aggregate. Toss and serve.

Serves 1. Time required for total preparation: 10 minutes

Each serving has an estimated: calories: 424 / total fat: 18.7g / carbohydrates: fifty two.3g / fiber: five.1g / protein:

Chapter 6 : Dinner

Clams chowder

This hearty chowder will surprise you, as it is completely alkaline friendly. The key to a traditional clam chowder is the presence of salty, chewy clams mixed into a thick cream base. In this recipe, we replace the clams with shiitake mushrooms, add some nori seaweed for that ocean flavor, and surround those in a thickened cream-like broth. Make this on those cold, winter days to soothe your heart and health.

Ingredients:

For the mushroom clams:

- ½ c kind of chopped shiitake mushrooms1 tsp. coconut oil¼ c water½ tsp. celery seed
- For the soup base
- ½ medium onion, chopped3 medium carrots, peeled and chopped2 celery stalks, finely chopped1 tsp. dried thyme3 c vegetable broth1 sheet nori, finely crumbled

For the cream base:

- 1 c gently steamed cauliflower¾ c unsweetened almond milk¼ tsp. sea salt
- To make the mushroom clams:
- In a huge pot set over medium excessive heat, upload the mushrooms and the coconut oil. Sauté for three mins. Add the water and celery seed, stirring till the water is absorbed. Take out from the high temperature and relocate the mushrooms to a plate.

To make the soup base:

- In the equal pot over medium warmth, sauté the onion, carrots, celery, and thyme for about 5 mins, or till the onion is softened. Add a number of the broth, if needed. Then, upload any last broth and the norm and produce it to a boil.
- To make the cream base:

Method:

1. In a mixer or food processor, add the cauliflower, almond milk, and salt. Blend to combine. If the mixture is too thick, upload some of the soup bases to thin. Blend until smooth.
2. To bring together the chowder:
3. Add the mushroom blend and the cream base to the soup base. Stir nicely to mix.

Heat for five minutes, or till warm, and serve.

Serves 4. Time required for total preparation: 15 minutes. Time required for thorough cooking:: 30 minutes
Each serving has an estimated (1 c): calories: 97 / total fat: 3.2g / carbohydrates: 10.8g / fiber: 2.4g /protein: 6.5g

Lovers' lasagna

Bet you're surprised there's a lasagna recipe in this cookbook! With zucchini strips as the noodles and a delicious White Sauce, you can have your lasagna and your healthy eating plan, too. The key to great taste is roasting the zucchini for a few minutes so it doesn't make the recipe soggy.

Ingredients:

- Four zucchini, sliced lengthwise into ¼-inch noodles
- 1 c Sun-Dried Tomato Sauce
- 1 c White Sauce

Method:

1. Preheat the oven to 350°F.
2. Place the zucchini noodles on a baking sheet and into the preheated oven. Roast for 10 minutes, then get rid of the oven.
3. In a small lasagna pan, cowl the lowest with one layer of zucchini strips. Top that with ¼ c Sun-Dried Tomato Sauce. Add some other layer of zucchini strips, placed crosswise from the primary layer. Top with another ¼ c Sun-Dried Tomato Sauce. Lay the 3rd layer of zucchini crosswise from the second layer and some other ¼ c Sun-Dried Tomato Sauce. Repeat with the last zucchini and ¼ c Sun-Dried Tomato Sauce.
4. Top the completed lasagna with the White Sauce. Cover with aluminum foil, the region the pan in the preheated oven, and bake for 15 minutes, or till hot and bubbly.
5. Take out from the stove and leave for few minutes before serving.

Serves 2. Time required for total preparation: 10 minutes. Time required for thorough cooking:: 25 minutes

Each serving has an estimated (½ finished recipe): calories: 184 / total fat: 3.6g / carbohydrates: 16.1g / fiber: 4.6g / protein: 5.4g

Stuffed peppers

This quick and clean recipe is also very elegant searching. The colorful peppers combine with the colors of the vegetables and quinoa to make it appearance restaurant worthy. It's excessive in fiber, excessive in protein, and high in deliciousness. The leftovers are a terrific lunch to take to work the next day, too.

Ingredients:

- Cooking spray
- 1 tsp. coconut oil
- ½ c chopped greens, zucchini, carrots, or broccoli
- 1 c cooked quinoa
- 1 tsp. garlic powder
- 1 tsp. onion powder
- 1 tsp. of sea salt
- Bell peppers, any shade, cored and seeded; tops removed and reserved.

Method:

1. Preheat the oven to 350°F.
2. Coat a baking pan with cooking spray.
3. In a medium saucepan set over medium warmness, upload the coconut oil and chopped greens. Sauté for five mins, or until softened.
4. Add the quinoa, garlic powder, onion powder, and salt. Stir to combine.

5. Place every bell pepper upright within the organized pan. Fill each pepper with one-1/2 of the quinoa-vegetable mix. Top every pepper with its reserved top.
6. Cover with aluminum foil, place inside the preheated oven, and bake for 15 minutes, or until the peppers are smooth.

Serves 2. Time required for total preparation: 5 minutes. Time required for thorough cooking:: 20 minutes

Each serving has an estimated (1 stuffed pepper): calories: 213 / total fat: 5.1g / carbohydrates: 34.8g / fiber: 5.5g / protein: 7.2g

Curried eggplant

This relatively clean dish is also healthy and scrumptious. It's an amazing idea to hold a broiled eggplant accessible because it's so easy to make, and you'll constantly have an ingredient accessible to make a brief meal.

Ingredients:

- 1 roasted eggplant, cooled, with contents removed from the shell and reserved
- Juice of 1 lemon
- 1 tsp. of sea salt
- 1 tsp. sesame oil
- 1 tsp. curry powder
- Water, as wanted
- Cooked quinoa, for serving

Method:

1. In a food processor, combine the eggplant, lemon juice, salt, sesame oil, and curry powder. Blend till easy.

2. To a small saucepan set over medium heat, switch the eggplant combination and warm it for about 5 mins. Add a few water to thin, if essential.

3. Serve as is, or over quinoa (if using).

4. To roast eggplant, truly slice it, upload a little sea salt, and bake in a 300°F oven for an approximate half-hour, or till it's smooth. Or, you can roast it whole as referred to as for right here. However, it's going to need to cook dinner a piece longer depending on the size, until it's without problems pierced with a sharp knife. Refrigerate till equipped to use.

Serves 2. Time required for total preparation: 5 mins. Time required for thorough cooking:: five mins

Each serving has an estimated (½ finished recipe): calories: eighty one / total fat: 2.8g / carbohydrates: 14.1g / fiber: 8.4g / protein: 2.4g

Championship chili

Few matters are better for looking at the game than a huge bowl of chili. This version takes all the hearty, familiar flavors and combines them right into a healthy meal. Using sprouted beans facilitates to decrease the alkalinity. Make a double batch and freeze the leftovers— when you have any! Be certain to apply diced tomatoes and pasta sauce that comprise no sugar, meat, or dairy.

Recipe Tip Fresh cilantro and dried cilantro have hugely distinctive flavors. If you don't have clean accessible, omit it altogether from the recipe.

Ingredients:

- Cooking spray
- 1 small onion, chopped
- 1 c diced red bell pepper
- garlic cloves, finely chopped
- c sprouted beans (see here), black, kidney, or pinto
- 1 (14.Five-oz.) can diced tomatoes
- 2 T Homemade Barbecue Sauce (right here)
- 1 (8-oz.) jar organic pasta sauce
- ¼ c organic salsa, mild, medium, or hot
- ¼ c organic fresh cilantro
- Dash chili powder
- Dash ground cumin

Method:

1. Spray a medium-length pot with cooking spray. Set it over medium warmth. Add the onions and sauté for 5 mins, or until they're tender and slightly caramelized.
2. Add the bell pepper, garlic, sprouted beans, tomatoes, Homemade Barbecue Sauce, pasta sauce, salsa, cilantro, chili powder, and cumin. Stir to combine. Simmer for 20 minutes.
3. Serve immediately.

Serves four. Time required for total preparation: 5 minutes. Time required for thorough cooking:: 25 minutes

Each serving has an estimated (1 c): calories: one hundred and one / total fat: 2.7g / carbohydrates: 18.5g / fiber: five.3g /protein: 3.9g